THE FUTURE OF US-PAKISTAN RELATIONS

We are fighting a war against a far-reaching network of hatred and violence . . . The front line of this fight is Afghanistan and Pakistan, where we are . . . strengthening the security and capacity of our partners.

—National Security Strategy, May 2010[1]

Since the tragic events of 9/11, Pakistan has achieved a central importance in United States (US) foreign policy not seen since the Soviet withdrawal from neighboring Afghanistan in 1989. Throughout the current operations in Afghanistan, Pakistan has been seen as vital to achieving anti-terror objectives and establishing regional stability.

Yet, its domestic and regional issues – and how they have manifested themselves – have been as heavily scrutinized as the quality of its efforts. Thus, the inevitable question emerges: why is Pakistan so important to achieving US goals in Afghanistan and overall stability in the South Asia? In "An Appraisal of the Afghanistan-Pakistan Strategy to Counter-Terrorism," Malik Zafar Iqbal states that "the tragic events of 9/11 . . . once again thrust Pakistan to the forefront of US strategy . . . Interests of both countries converged."[2] Yet, US Army War College Professor Larry P. Goodson more directly states: "Pakistan is one of only nine states . . . known to have nuclear weapons . . . (and is the) epicenter of Islamist extremism."[3] Thus, one can understand its strategic importance to the US.

Yet, converging interests and conditions can create obstacles and pressures that alter policy, behavior and perceptions of their coherency. The US and the West are studying Pakistan's efforts in this light to optimize relations and create more appropriate regional policies. Throughout the 10-year Afghan operations, Pakistan's efforts have been perceived by some as often confusing, contradictory, and outright counter-productive. Yet, to understand its behavior, one needs to understand Pakistan itself and the driving forces behind its policies and behavior.

This paper will focus on the following question: what are the most important factors driving Pakistan's foreign policy and behavior and what can be done to favorably influence them? While there are numerous impacting determinants, this study will focus on two. The first is *India-Pakistan (Indo-Pak) relations* and how the unresolved Kashmir dispute influences it. The second will concern *Ideology*, and how Islamic extremism and ethno-linguistic aspects have influenced its application in Pakistan's affairs. To effectively analyze them depends on understanding the nature and evolution of Pakistan itself – a standpoint from which this analysis will start. Understanding these factors may not only provide insight on the driving forces behind Pakistan's policies and behaviors as well as clues on how to address its domestic and regional concerns. Positively affecting them could result in improved US-Pakistan (US-Pak) relations and regional stability.

Pakistan: An Overview

The dissolution of the British Raj (i.e., British India) in 1947 resulted in the Union of India. The subsequent partition of India ignited communal violence, displaced an estimated 12.5 million people, [4] and led to two sovereign nations – India and Pakistan. While India emerged as a largely Hindu state, Pakistan became an Islamic-secular nation. Pakistan covers approximately 796,095 square kilometers (i.e., 310,410 square miles) or almost twice the size of California, [5] and has a population of approximately 177.3 million (95% Muslim, or 75% Sunni and 15-20% Shia). The "Pakistan at a Glance" table (*Figure 1*)[6] provides a general overview of Pakistan's major facets.

Despite its Islamic majority, Pakistan is considered to be a federal parliamentary republic, consisting of four provinces: Balochistan (largest in land area; population of 12 million); Khyber-Pakhtunkhwa (i.e., North-West Frontier Province until 2010), which contains the Swat valley; the Punjab; and Sindh.[7] It also contains four recognized territories:

Pakistan at a Glance

Population: 177 million; growth rate: 1.5% (2010 est.)
Area: 803,940 sq. km. (slightly less than twice the size of California)
Capital: Islamabad
Heads of Government: Prime Minister Yousaf Raza Gilani and President Asif Ali Zardari (both of the Pakistan People's Party)
Ethnic Groups: Punjabi 45%, Pashtun 15%, Sindhi 14%, Saraiki 8%, Muhajir 8%. Baloch 4%, other 6%
Languages: Punjabi 48%, Sindhi 12%, Saraiki 10%, Pashtu 8%, Urdu (official) 8%; Baluchi, English (official), and others 14%
Religions: Muslim 95% (Sunni 75%, Shia 20%), Christian, Hindu, and other 5%
Life Expectancy at Birth: female 67 years; male 64 years (2010 est.)
Literacy: 50% (female 36%; male 63%; 2005 est.)
Gross Domestic Product (at PPP): $449 billion; per capita: $2,600; growth rate 2.7% (2009 est.)
Currency: Rupee (100 = $1.17)
Inflation: 13.2% (1st quarter 2010)
Defense Budget: $4.11 billion (2.6% of GDP; 2009)
U.S. Trade: exports to U.S. $3.2 billion (primarily textiles and apparel); imports from U.S. $1.6 billion (incl. raw cotton and military equipment) (2009)

Figure 1: Pakistan at a Glance
(Source: K. Alan Kronstadt's "Pakistan: Key Current Issues and Developments")

capital territory (i.e., Islamabad's location); Federally Administered Tribal Agencies (FATA); and two northern mountainous regions, known as Gilbit-Baltistan (i.e., the Northern Areas until 2009), and Azad (or "free) Kashmir."

These territories are "centered on a major ethno-linguistic group that is primarily located in that province,"[8] and form the cultural affiliations and ideological/ethno-linguistic influences that impact its governance. Due in part to its rugged topography, there is relative isolation between each province, facilitating the development of exclusive cultures and tribes. For example, the Punjab (meaning "'land of the five rivers" in Persian) is occupied by roughly 71 million Punjabis, comprising 75% of its total population.[9] The Sindh, more varied in population than the Punjab, contains approximately 38 million people, over 60% of which are Sindhi-speakers. The presence of Pakistan's second largest city, Karachi, might account for the population variety, as it is has been a focal point for migration throughout the subcontinent.[10] In addition to its Sindh-speaking population, Karachi contains over 9 million *Muhajirs* and over one million Afghan refugees.[11]

3

Perhaps the most extensive example of cultural or ethno-linguistic provincial isolation involves the seven tribal areas of the Federally-Administered Tribal Areas (FATA), which are: Kyber, Kurram, Orakzai, Mohamand, Bajur, and North and South Waziristan.[12] All reside on the Afghanistan-Pakistan (AF-Pak) border, known as the "Durand Line" and, as will be demonstrated later, are virtual breeding grounds for Islamist *Jihadis* who play a direct role in the current hostilities.

Adding to the demographic complexity is the fact that over 20 languages are spoken in Pakistan. The most common are: Punjabi (48% of the population), Sindhi (12%), and Urdu – which is the official national language but is spoken by only 8% of the population (i.e., people who identify themselves as muhajirs). Other languages include: Siraiki, which is a Punjabi variant (10%), Pakhtu or Pashton (8%), Balochi (3%), Hindko (2%), Brahuci (1%), other languages (8%).[13] This language diversity reflects Pakistan's insular ethnic group composition, complicating its already intricate demographic profile.

The country's provincial, tribal, and ethno-linguistic breakdown directly impacts Pakistani politics. Since Independence in 1947, Pakistan's secular governments have been largely unstable and short-lived. In its 64 years of existence, Pakistan has had over 24 changes in leadership, with over 84 political parties involved in its political process. Overall, it has had "(35 years) of military rule . . . (33 years of) civilian leadership under . . . numerous political systems."[14] Currently, there are over 23 major parties – the most prominent being the *Pakistan People's Party* (*PPP*) and divisions of the *Pakistan Muslim League* (*PML*). However, there are several province-based parties extensively involved in representing local interests, including the *Balochistan National Party-Awami* (*BNP-A*). The Pakistani constitution has been suspended and revised approximately nine times since 1973. There have been numerous coups, including those by army chief general Ayub

Khan (1958), General Yayha Kahn (1969), Zia ul Haq (1977), and General Pervez Musharraf (1999). Additionally, the hanging of Zulfikar Ali Bhutto (1979) and assassination of his daughter, former Prime Minister Benazir Bhutto on December 27, 2007, are added examples of the oft-violent instability plaguing Pakistani politics.

When it does work, Pakistan's federal republic is run by a bicameral parliament (i.e., *Majlis-e-Shoora*) consisting of a Senate (100 seats, indirectly elected by provincial assemblies and territorial representatives) and "the National Assembly (342 seats; 272 members elected by popular vote)."[15] In addition to the afore-mentioned ethnic and provincial influences, there are several political "pressure groups" that exert significant influences. Foremost among them are: the army/military (most influential), ulema (clergy), and land owners (i.e., "Feudalists").

The Pakistani military is the eighth largest in the world and is one of nine nations to possess nuclear weapons capability. Currently, the Pakistani military consists of the following personnel strengths: Army – 550,000 (Active Duty); Navy – 22,000; Air Force – 45,000 (350 Aircraft), amounting to approximately 617,000 total personnel.[16] Its power and influence are rooted in its alliances with feudal landowners, Pakistan's Inter-services Intelligence (ISI) bureau, and popular support.

The army is also a major contributor to the agriculture-based Pakistani economy. For example, the army owns two of the country's largest conglomerates: *Fauzi Foundation* and *Army Welfare Trust (AWT)*. The *Fauzi Foundation* owns sugar mills, chemical plants, fertilizer factories, gas and power plants, over 800 schools and 100 or more hospitals. The *AWT* has over $1 billion in assets, and also owns the Askari Bank – one of the largest banks in Pakistan. Although it owns few charitable ventures, it does pay over half of its income to finance army pensions. It also owns the Pakistani *Special Communication Organization*, which supplies telecommunications in Pakistani-held parts of Kashmir."[17]

Enhancing the military's overarching influence are the "ulama" (also spelled "Ulema," which is singular). They are Islamic clergy or Muslim religious scholars involved in several fields of Islamic study, and who exercise their authority under Islam to effect political or social changes. Arbiters of *Shari'a Law,* they hold relative authority over Mullahs and Imams, giving them potent ideological influence within Islam-centered agencies, including tribal areas and government bureaus. The *ulama* enhance the military's influence "because of their armed militias and their contribution to the Army's crucial agenda of keeping the Kashmir issue alive. They exercise considerable coercive and ideological control over civil society. Their leverage on the Government is far more palpable than that of the politicians. It is no surprise, therefore, that they have asserted their agenda very aggressively . . . They want a change in foreign policy that even the hawkish establishment in Islamabad cannot implement . . . (and) have announced their decision . . . to gain power on the basis of militant Islamic ideology."[18] Pakistan's political system contains several "ulema-based" parties, including *Jamiat Ulema-e-Pakistan (JUP)* [19] and the *Jamiat-Ulema-e-Islam Fazl,* demonstrating a political as well as military impact.

And, finally, another influence – perhaps the greatest cause of socio-economic disparity in Pakistan – is the existence of "feudalist" or multi-generational land owners. This group collectively owns over 75% of the country's agricultural capability, which represents over 23% of (Pakistan's) GDP and 44% of (its) jobs.[20]

According to Owen Bennett Jones, "the classic (Feudalists) are the major landowners in Southern Punjab and Sindh (and) derive their power . . . by . . . the sheer size of their estates...Feudal leaders of Sindh and Punjab and the tribal leaders who hold sway in Baluchistan . . . and NWFP (and) . . . differ in authority. For example, tribal leaders do not have unquestioned authority, nor can they be certain that their power will pass to their sons."[21] In other terms, the Feudalists hold economic and thus cultural and political power within the provinces and tribal areas – further enhancing the isolation and thus hindering nation-building and unity in Pakistan. They exercise authority outside of government institutions, including adjudicating legal claims (driven by popular mistrust of the Pakistani court system) in their lands and even issuing marriage licenses. [22]

The "Feudalists" generally protect their interests in Parliament. For example, no Pakistani government has been able to levy a tax on agriculture, the primary source of feudal wealth. Overall, the feudalists preserve their power by preventing comprehensive socio-economic development or reforms in their areas, effectively ensuring a clear hierarchy over a distant or distinct "middle class."[23] Past and current military and civilian leaders each recognize that feudal areas are large obstacles to development. Yet, ethno-tribal insulation in tribal and other areas ensures the preservation of their culture, ideas, and overall existence.[24] Collectively, these influences have significantly hindered efforts to establish a consistently effective or stable civilian-secular government.

Despite these constraints, Pakistan's agriculture-based economy has experienced 5-8% GDP growth, attributable to gains in the industrial and service sectors since 2005. As of 2010, it has a total GDP of $464.9B (#28 in the world) and has extensive trade relations with China (17.9%), Saudi Arabia (10.7%), United Arab Emirates (UAE) (10.6%), Kuwait (5.5%), and the US (4.9%). However, approximately 24% of its population is below the poverty line.[25] This is due primarily to the feudalist influence and its adverse effects on Pakistan's small middle class, which include the absence of the socio-economic reforms needed for upward mobility in Pakistan's economic class structure.

History

As indicated earlier, one needs to understand a country's nature, history, and development to recognize and analyze the factors driving its policies and conduct. From the very beginning, Pakistan has been a land continuously intersected by various religious and urban cultures, and political traditions.

Modern day Pakistan covers most of the territory occupied by the ancient Indus Valley civilization (3300-1200 BCE), which occupied the land centuries before the evolution of Hinduism and other regional religious-political traditions. Its history is punctuated by frequent cultural displacement by various invaders, including expeditions by Alexander the Great (356-323 BCE) – which was prompted by Greek and Persian rivalries in the region. Migrations to the Indus Valley led to the presence of three major religions in the area: Buddhism, Hinduism, and Islam (brought by Muslim Arabs – and *ulama* – in the 8th century). The Mughal Empire era (1526-1857) saw the entrance of European and later British occupation the Indian subcontinent. [26]

Following the "Indian Rebellion" in 1857 – and territorial cessation from the British East India Company to the British Empire – the Pakistani "modernist" movement began in the late 19th century. It was led by Sir Syed Ahmed Khan (1817-98), an academic receptive to "western scientific conceptions who sought to develop a separate Muslim political creed."[27]

However, in *Deadly Embrace*, former Obama Administration advisor, Bruce Riedel, writes: "the idea of Pakistan was . . . born in the 1930's (when) a student at Cambridge University, Chaudhary Rahmat Ali, envisioned a Muslim state created from the union of several British-controlled territories . . . of the subcontinent. He (called) this new state . . . "Pakistan" . . . (which is) basically an acronym compiled from the (area) names of the

8

Punjab, Afghania, Kashmir, Sindh, and Baluchistan. In Persian and Urdu, Pakistan also translates as 'the land of the pure.'"[28] As a side note, the only province omitted from the acronym was East Pakistan (later Bangladesh), foreshadowing difficulties to come.

Unsurprisingly, numerous religious and political groups in India opposed the idea, envisioning a unified, all-inclusive nation regardless of religion. However, the "Movement for Pakistan," as it was soon called, gained momentum in the subcontinent and the United Kingdom (UK), where even Prime Minister Winston Churchill encouraged the creation of Pakistan (yet some speculate his efforts were to spite Mohatma Gandhi for his civil disobedience in British India in the 1930's-40s).

However, in spite of Western influences, the true prime mover for Pakistan "in South Asia was Muhammad Ali Jinnah, also known as Baba-e-Quam (the father of the country) or Quaid-e-Azam (the great leader). Jinnah and his Muslim League Party spearheaded the drive to independence."[29]

On July 18, 1947, the passage of the *Indian Independence Act* in 1947 led to the dissolution of India and creation of both India and Pakistan on August 15, 1947. The subsequent partition later that year created the need for affected Hindus, Sikhs, and Muslims to find new homes. This led to "one of the largest refugee transfers in history," with over 12 million displaced (and over one million deaths). The "aftershocks of that division" still impact the region and world today.[30]

Muhammad Ali Jinnah – a British lawyer – seemed like an unlikely candidate to essentially create the world's first Muslim state. To contemporaries and later biographers, he was not known for his religious piety. Although a *Shia* Muslim (a minority in Islam, as over 90% of Muslims – including those in Pakistan today – are *Sunni*), he was a dedicated smoker (smoking over fifty cigarettes a day), consumed alcohol, and had more than 200

9

high-priced Savile row business suits. One year, the *New York Times* named him one of the

"ten best dressed men of the British Empire. He also unsuccessfully ran for the British

Parliament in 1930 . . . As his Indian biographer, Jaswant Singh, put it: 'Jinnah was

committed to his three-piece suits, his lorgnette, his cigarette holder, and the King's

English.'"[31]

Still, he laid out the vision comprising the Ideological and political basis for Pakistani

governance:

> You are free, free to go to your mosques or to any other places of worship in this state of Pakistan. You may belong to any religion or caste or creed that has nothing to do with the business of the state . . . In the course of time Hindus would cease to be Hindus and Muslims would cease to the Muslims, not in the religious sense, because that is the personal faith of each individual, but in the political sense as citizens of the state.[32]

In other terms, Islam was to be used as an instrument to establish cultural and

eventually national unity. As Riedel notes, "Jinnah's vision was not rooted in religious

piety . . . Rather, (his) great concern was that a united India would treat its Muslims as

second-class citizens, persecuted by the Hindu majority . . . He saw a separate Pakistan

as a haven where they could practice their religion to whatever degree of piety they

desired. Founded for Muslims, it would not be a secular state but would . . . act like one in

advocating tolerance and diversity."[33]

His vision also discouraged discrimination or extremism of any kind. However, he

did not live long enough to see his vision become a reality. He died on September 11,

1948 of Tuberculosis and lung cancer. Because he had not named or prepared any

potential successor, his death left a leadership vacuum. The 1951 assassination of

Jinnah's chief lieutenant and successor, Liaquat Ali Khan, set the stage for political

instability that continues to this day.[34]

In October 1958, eight-year Army chief of staff, Major General Ayub Khan, led the first of four military coups that toppled Pakistan's civilian-led government. On assuming power, he quickly abrogated the constitution, banned political parties, and named himself president. "Among the several reasons for his coup . . . was the fear that a truly democratic election would tilt the balance of power toward East Pakistan at the expense of the army-dominated west."[35] This motive was symptomatic of increasing East-West Pakistan tensions, foreshadowing future developments.

Under Khan, Pakistan underwent several changes designed to consolidate power and exercise greater control over the loyalties and agencies within the government. For example, "the Inter-Services Intelligence Directorate (ISI) grew in size and importance. Founded by British Major General William Cawthorne at Independence . . . the ISI now took on the role of spying on Ayub's enemies inside Pakistan. It would be the beginning of the ISI's rise to power."[36] Khan also staged many "elections," including the 1965 election when he was "officially" elected president. His opponent was Jinnah's sister, Fatima, who – like others – accused Khan of using patronage and intimidation to influence the vote. This repression of democracy further exacerbated tensions throughout the country.[37]

By 1968, Khan relinquished power due to popular discontent with his government, which was viewed as corrupt. He relinquished power to General Agha Mohammad Yahya Khan Qizilbash (or Yahya Khan), who got off to a sub-stellar start by immediately imposing Martial Law to suppress what he believed to be disorder. According to Riedel, Yahya Khan "proved a disaster for Pakistan."[38] For example, conscious of Bengali anger in East Pakistan, Yahya tried to appease them by bringing more Bengalis into the Army (as there were only 300 officers in the entire Army) and holding free elections. However, when the independence-leaning Bengali Party, the *Awami League* gained a majority in Pakistan's

11

National Assembly by winning 160 of 162 seats, the Punjabi became concerned with Bengali domination and essentially pushed the country into civil war.

Operation Searchlight, conducted in March 1971, was initiated to crack down on the East and decapitate its leadership. The operation reportedly killed over 3 million people and led to various atrocities. This also led to an East-West split in Pakistan, aided by Indian intervention to support the new Bangladesh (Bengali) resistance. In December 1971, Yayha launched a preemptive strike on Indian airbases and radar stations. "Dubbed *Operation Genghis Khan*, (it led to) the Third Indo-Pakistani War"[39] (the other two -in 1947 and 1965 - were fought over Kashmir and will be addressed later). The Pakistani army was badly beaten, with over 90,000 soldiers surrendering to India on December 16, 1971.[40] The surrender constituted the largest number of prisoners of war taken since World War II. The debacle forced Yayha's resignation and transfer of power to Zulfikar Ali Bhutto, a former foreign minister and leader of the Pakistan's Peoples Party (PPP).

The ascension of Bhutto restored civilian-secular government after two tumultuous decades. However, the military was too fully ingrained in Pakistani politics to allow him the freedom necessary to institute needed bureaucratic and socio-economic reforms. For example, the contrasting vision and ambitions of the military effectively undermined his "Islamic Socialism" socio-economic reform initiative, which advocated the redistribution of wealth based on the conceptions of the Islamic prophet Muhammad.

However, Bhutto's most enduring legacy was establishing the Pakistani nuclear program – something that would cause significant US-Pak and regional tensions. "On January 24, 1972, in a secret meeting with the nation's scientific elite in the city of Multan, Bhutto ordered them...to build a bomb. Pakistan, he commanded, must get a bomb even if it meant Pakistanis had to starve and 'eat grass.'"[41] Aided by China and Russia, Pakistan

12

eventually developed and tested its first atomic bomb in 1998 – forever changing the strategic calculus of South Asia.

After allegations of election tampering, Bhutto's Army chief of staff, Muhammad Zia Ul-Haq, deposed him in a coup on July 5, 1977. He was arrested on questionable charges of murder and corruption, and hanged on April 4, 1979.

Ideologically, Zia was the most influential Pakistani leader since Jinnah. While Jinnah's vision brought secular and democratic aspirations, "it was (Zia ul-Haq)," according to Ziad Haider, "who would (convert) Pakistan to an Islamic state."[42] Specifically, Zia's tenure (which ended when he died in a plane crash on August 17, 1988) would seismically shift Pakistani governance to a focus on religious obscurantism and inclusion of Islam into all levels of government and the already-suspect judiciary.

Describing himself as a "soldier of Islam," he provided the following vision:

> Pakistan, which was created in the name of Islam, will continue to survive only if it sticks to Islam. That is why I consider the introduction of Islamic systems as an essential prerequisite for the country.[43]

While the transformational aspects of Zia's rule will be addressed later, it stands that his inclusion of Islamic precepts and mechanisms into national governance further distorted Jinnah's vision of secular and Islamic principals working in complement to create a coherent national identity and stable governance. Instead, Zia's vision paid lip service to democratic/secular principals but his way of achieving them was through theocratic instruments, creating compatibility challenges.

On December 24, 1979, the Soviet Union invaded Afghanistan, bringing a fundamental shift in regional stability. The event brought a new chapter in US-Pak relations, as both nations established a closer military-intelligence effort to defeat the Soviets. In addition to supplying military supply routes into Afghanistan, the US-Pakistani intelligence relationship "became a trilateral one between the (Central Intelligence Agency) CIA, ISI, and (Saudi General Intelligence Directorate) GID in which Washington and Riyadh provided matching grants of money and purchased arms, while Islamabad handled distribution and training . . . No more than a hundred people were involved . . . (perhaps making it) one of the most cost-effective programs ever run by the US government."[44] However, Zia's death led to another experiment in secular/democratic governance with the election (in June 1988) of Benazir Bhutto – Zulfikar Bhutto's oldest daughter and leader of the PPP.

Benazir Bhutto (1953-2007) was the 11th Prime Minister in Pakistan's history (since 1947) and the first female leader of an Islamic country. Serving two non-consecutive terms (i.e., 1988-90 and 1993-96), she professed western-style, socialist approaches to socio-economic reforms and industrial development- generally promoting a variation of the "Islamic-Socialism" favored by her father. However, haunted by the deaths of her father and younger brother, Murtza (after an encounter with Sindh police in 1996), she maintained an uneasy relationship with the Army at best and was always suspicious of the ISI, whom she thought was out to overthrow her.

Her tenures in office, both ending with dismissals by then-President Ghulam Ishaq, were marked by the Soviet withdrawal from Afghanistan and the massive refugee migration that followed, which strained US-Pak relations. She believed that the US had abandoned Pakistan after the withdrawal, forcing it to deal with the refugees alone. US-Pak relations were further strained by its nuclear program. However, her administration – and that of Nawaz Sharif afterward – brought Pakistan one of its longest periods of civilian-government control since its independence.

On October 12, 1999, the omnipresent tension between the military and civilian government erupted again when Army chief of staff, General Pervez Musharraf came to power in a bloodless coup – sending Bhutto into exile.[45] Originally designated as "Chief Executive," he later named himself as President in 2001. Musharraf's tenure spanned most of the decade and, because of 9/11, brought renewed cooperation with the US. It also saw Pakistan's internal animosities and instability – driven by escalating domestic and regional pressures – be brought to light. It would invite more scrutiny of Pakistan's veracity and capacities as an ally in support of the US-led operations in Afghanistan.

This instability was typified by the events of Musharraf's tenure[46], which included: surviving two assassination attempts (2003); resumption of Indo-Pak nuclear talks after three years (suspended after the 2001 attack on the Indian Parliament, which was allegedly conducted by Pakistani extremists); occurrence over "211 (270 through 2009) suicide bomber attacks through 2008"[47]; a magnitude 7.6 earthquake in Azad Pakistan, killing tens of thousands in the region and leaving over 3 million people homeless; and occurrence of over "98 unmanned aerial drone strikes in Pakistan through 2008 (and over 280 drone strikes through 2011, with over 94.3% occurring in North and South Waziristan)."[48] His tenure also saw the "Red Mosque" gun battle (in Islamabad), which killed 43 people.

Perhaps the turning point in his tenure was when PPP leader (and rival) Benazir Bhutto returned to Pakistan after nine years in exile in October 2007. Only hours after she arrived in Karachi, 140 people were killed by a bomb blast (Bhutto was unhurt). Although Musharraf denied any complicity in the event, emerging suspicions put more pressure on his increasingly unsteady time in office. Two months later, Bhutto was assassinated and about 20 others were killed at a political rally in Rawalpindi, threatening to spark country-

15

wide chaos (2007). Her husband, Asif Ali Zardari, was named as her successor. Suspicion over Musharraf's involvement in Bhutto-s assassination – and curtailment of civil and media rights in May 2007 (citing threats from militants) led to his party's defeat in the 2008 Parliamentary elections. Facing impeachment, Musharraf resigned in August 2008, with Zardari taking over as Prime Minister.

Since 2008, Zardari has served as Prime Minister of an increasingly unstable country. With the US raid into Pakistani territory on May 1, 2011 that killed 9/11 terrorist Osama bin Laden (at his compound in Abbottabad) and the additional number of aerial drone strikes into Pakistan, US-Pak relations have become increasingly strained. Yet, the status of US-Pak relations is yet another product of the various domestic and regional factors - including Indo-Pak relations and Ideology - impacting its way of doing business. The unresolved factors so prevalent in its history continue to cloud its present.

Factor One: Indo-Pak Relations

For centuries, the ancestors of today's Indians and Pakistanis shared the same land and resources, and were shaped by the same influences – from the 300-year rule of the Mughal Empire to the Persian, Greece, Central Asian, and European migrations. These combined to create the complex ethno-linguistic profile and array of cultures that define the subcontinent today. Yet, despite this existential kinship, India and Pakistan are competing and contending sovereigns – indeed, bitter enemies currently embroiled in regional nuclear competition and the longest ongoing territorial dispute (i.e., Kashmir). How did the situation become so intractable and volatile, despite their common heritage? The answer, in part, lies in two underlying facets: the partition and the Kashmir dispute.

For a "trigger point" of Indo-Pak instability, one needs to look first at the 1947 partition (described earlier), primarily driven by the Indian nationalist movements of the

16

19th century while the territory was still under the rule of the British East India Company and the empire itself. The 1947 Indian Independence brought the 350-year British occupation to an end. Yet, although "the British, the (*Indian National*) *Congress*, the *Muslim League* . . . and *All-India Muslim Conference* were responsible"[49] for the Indian division, none understood its potentially devastating effects. They also appeared to underestimate the passions – and resulting perspectives – that had been developing since the late 19th century, based on the collective historic memory. Shirin Keen relates:

> By the late 19th century there were . . . communal conflicts and movements in the country that were based on religious communities rather than class or regional ones. Some people felt that the very nature of Islam called for a communal Muslim society. Added to this were the memories of power over the Indian subcontinent that the Muslims held on to . . . (during) Mughal rule. These memories might have made it exceptionally difficult for Muslims to accept the imposition of colonial power and culture.[50]

Thus, the partition left the subcontinent devastated, with millions of refugees pouring into unfamiliar regions and, like those in Pakistan today, populations had become embedded in regions (and cultures) isolated from the collective national identity. The partition claimed the lives of Hindus, Muslims and Sikhs alike.[51]

The impacts of the partition were profound, changing the entire dynamic of South Asia. Many of the displaced cultures are still trying to find their identities after leaving regions they had occupied for centuries. Both Pakistan and India existed for decades in abject poverty, as the partition ruined their economies – including industrial and agricultural capabilities – and occurred without functional systems of government. Several pivotal Indians and Pakistanis who engineered the separation, including Gandhi, Jinnah and Allama Iqbal, died soon afterward – leaving the region without viable leadership. The ethnic unrest that started with the partition ultimately resulted in the 1971 secession of

Bangladesh from Pakistan. Today, the partition's affects are still felt in both countries, with unresolved ethnic, ideological/religious, and territorial issues remaining.

If the partition was the "trigger," the Kashmir dispute has become the epicenter – or "center of gravity"– for Indo-Pak instability and overall relations. Its resolution – or lack thereof – has become the driving force behind security and foreign policy decisions for both nations.

The term "Kashmir" refers to the Indian state made up of Jammu, Azad Kashmir, and Ladakh, officially called "Jammu-Kashmir." However, the term "Kashmir" (or the "Valley of the Kashmir") is generally used to describe the whole region.

During the partition, India gained control of Jammu, Kashmir, and Ladakh provinces, while Pakistan gained control of Gilgit, Baltisan, and Azad Kashmir. Based on a border dispute with India, the Chinese seized control of the Aksai Chin (i.e., historic lands in Kashmir) in the 1950s. China and India fought a border war 1962 but China retained control. Today, India controls only 54,000 square miles of the territory; Pakistan has 32,000; China has less than 6,000.[52] It has a population of approximately 4.7 million people, most of which are Kashmir-speaking Sunni Muslims. However, the three divisions of Kashmir have dominant ethnic divisions that complicate the Indo-Pak dispute. For example, Jammu (south of the valley) contains a Hindu majority, while Azad (free) Kashmir (western – southern areas), has 3.1 million people – 90% of which are Muslim.[53]

Along with the religious and ethnic composition in Kashmir, another impetus behind the dispute is the control of resources in the valley – perhaps motivated by the abject poverty Pakistan more seriously experienced after the partition. For example, Jammu and Kashmir contain forests covering roughly "eight thousand square miles," affording materials for making furniture and other wood products. Metal ores (i.e., copper, Iron, zinc, and marble) and fresh water lakes, such as Dal Lake with its ecosystem of floating gardens and rich soils for fruits and vegetables, also exist.[54] These and other resources could have mitigated the hardships of both countries if shared equally. Indeed, while India's impacts were initially adverse, the resources contained in its Kashmir territories provided some means of recovery. Pakistan, however, did not receive those Muslim-dominated Kashmir territories to which it believed it was entitled.

According to Howard B. Schaffer, former US deputy assistant secretary of state for South Asian affairs, the essence of the dispute is this:

> Pakistanis perceive Kashmir as the one Muslim-majority area of Britain's Indian empire that did not become part of Pakistan, conceived by its founders as the homeland for Muslims of the subcontinent. (It) is 'the unfinished business of partition. For Indians, Kashmir's Muslim majority makes it a symbol of the country's secular identity. Losing Kashmir because it is Muslim would . . . undercut (India's) secular claims and confirm (the unacceptable) view that Hindus and Muslims . . . should have separate states.[55]

Thus, Kashmir remains the most long-standing and militarized international territorial dispute (although each country has maintained a cease-fire since 2004). Yet, related armed stand-offs present other challenges in the Siachen glacier region, India's militarized 450-mile (700 Km) "line of control (LOC)" (dividing Jammu and Kashmir from northeast Pakistan), and the border dispute in the Sir Creek estuary.

So, how have Indo-Pakistan relations – and specifically the issue of Kashmir – driven Pakistan's foreign policy decisions? Examples include:

- In 1947-48, Pakistan initiated "The Kashmir operation" to gain control of Kashmir, invoking "jihad to mobilize tribesmen from the frontier and send them to...seize Kashmir."[56] The operation failed, resulting in "India (getting) the bulk of the province. Pakistan held on to a smaller part, which it named Azad Kashmir, (or) "free Kashmir."[57]

- From April-September 1965, Pakistan initiated a series of skirmishes that ultimately escalated into a second war with India over Kashmir. Riedel relates: "Khan devised a plot code-named *Operation Gibraltar* to infiltrate Indian-held Kashmir with teams of Pakistanis who would foment an uprising (requiring) Pakistani intervention . . . A second maneuver, *Operation Grand Slam* . . . would strike into India to cut off Kashmir and win the war . . . The plan misfired badly. "[58]

- In 1974, India detonated its first atomic bomb. In response, Zulfikar Bhutto ordered the Pakistani military and scientific community to acquire a bomb at all costs (which it eventually did in 1998). Although Kashmir is not specifically linked to nuclear proliferation efforts, the wars and tensions caused by the dispute drove the capability development (from Pakistan's view) to ensure a more equal balance of power.

- In May and July 1999, Pakistani and Kashmir insurgents attacked the Kargil district in Kashmir and along the LOC, prompting counterattacks by Indian army patrols. Pakistan's Prime Minister and Chief of Army Staff and paramilitary forces, led by General Ashraf Rashid, led the assault. Under international opposition, the Pakistani forces eventually withdrew from the remaining Indian positions along the LOC.

- October 2001: Pakistan-based militants, *Jaish-e-Mohammed*, attacked the Kashmiri assembly in Srinagar (Kashmir's capital), killing 38 people. Two months later, Pakistani militants attacked the Indian parliament in New Delhi, killing 14 people.[59]

These major events exemplify not only the dispute but its intensity and regional implications. The Kashmir conflict has now become the focus of militants using Pakistan territory for safe harbor. And, as India strives to ensure its own domestic security, this "culmination point" conflict threatens to indirectly influence Indian involvement in Afghanistan as well. As Malik Zafar Iqbal writes, "India's increasing influence in

Afghanistan has been largely downplayed . . . it has . . . grown to the point where Pakistan no longer views its flanks as secure . . . increasing Indian influence in Afghanistan would probably aggravate the regional tensions and cause Pakistan to directly counter India's subterfuge in Afghanistan . . ."[60] This is yet another example of the impacts of Indo-Pak relations on Pakistan's foreign policy decisions.

The US must address the sources of Indo-Pak tensions to facilitate not only regional stability but achieve its own objectives as well. As Iqbal writes, "the (US) . . . should assuage the tension between India and Pakistan and actively pursue the resolution of the Kashmir issue"[61] if it is to be successful in its own operations in the Afghan-Pakistan region.

Factor Two: Ideology

While the Indo-Pak relationship compels policies to address conflict and security concerns, perhaps the most overarching causal factor impacting Pakistan's policy decisions and behavior is "Ideology" – defined as the fundamental structure of precepts establishing the values, perspectives, and identity of the nation. For Pakistan, this ideology is rooted in extremist interpretations of Islam.

As illustrated earlier, the partition – or separation of India into two sovereign nations – was predicated on Ideology. India believed in secular-democratic principles that included all religions, castes and creeds – existing together to comprise a unified and diverse national identity. In sum, Indian policy since independence insisted upon the inclusion of Muslims as well as Hindus and other religions. Conversely, Pakistan – as illustrated in Jinnah's and later Khan's visions – believed in establishing an Islamic-secular state, with Islam acting as the central instrument impelling national unity and identity. Thus, Ideology began to play a role in national decisions even before the Indian and Pakistani governments were fully established.

Today, Pakistan's existential basis – its Islamic ideology – has continued to be reinterpreted, misrepresented, or entirely polluted by numerous power-seekers and antagonists (among others). Complicated by its ethno-linguistic and/or tribal diversity – in which tribal leaders to feudalists have their own conceptions of Islam and what conduct is justified under it – Pakistan now presents a confusing Islam-based rationale for its policies and behavior.

Pakistan's ideological emphasis and development in 1947 reflected its history and societal experiences at the time. However, in 1947, simply using "Islam" an instrument to establish cultural and eventually national unity (i.e., Jinnah's vision) was insufficient to fully clarify exactly what set of ideas Pakistan's new rulers wanted to follow. For example, Muslims in India fell into two "traditions:" *Aligarh*, which generally embraced Western culture and notions of modernity; and, the *Deoband*, which rejected the West as deviating from religion.[62] Thus, these traditions followed separate secular and religious philosophies – even though they were technically "Islam." Overall, Jinnah never clarified "who's Islam" he intended to follow.

When the time came to establish an overarching "Islamic" ideological basis for Pakistan, the preceding traditions were at work throughout India – both approaching religious and cultural assimilation differently. Thus, what passed for "policy" among Indian Muslims at the time reflected the traditional divisions, creating assimilation challenges within Muslim communities. However, Jinnah believed that resolving at least the latter differences would occur in time in an Islamic-state and, for the time being, would have to be subordinated for political expediency.

Politically, India divided into three groups: *Indian Congressional Party* (dominated by Hindus); *All-Indian Muslim League* (led by Jinnah), "which contended that Muslims had a special identity that would be erased in a Hindu-majority India;"[63] and, various other religious groups that opposed a separate Muslim homeland. Of course, the Muslim league prevailed, and Pakistan was born.

The *Objectives Resolution of 1949* was meant to establish the principles for Pakistan's constitution and called for "the principles of democracy, freedom, equality, and tolerance as annunciated by Islam . . ."[64] Yet, despite Jinnah's intended purpose for Islam, (i.e., as a unifying cultural and national philosophy), there had never been a uniform vision of Pakistan. As Haider indicates, Pakistan was and "remains a product of contesting visions."[65]

This ideological fissure allowed Zia to essentially redefine the role of Islam and the dimensions of governance under it. His activities were transformational, as they not only changed Jinnah's governmental secular focus but also impacted the way Pakistan treated its societies and international partners. The *Deoband* rejection of the West became a more focused "us against them" proposition – all dictated by perhaps questionable interpretations of the Quran. Examples of Zia's transformational footprint include the following:

- The army's slogan was changed to: "Imam (father), Taqwa (piety), and Jihad fi Sabil Allah (Jihad for the Sake of God)."

- Evangelical groups like the *Tableeghi Jamat* linked to the *Deobandi* tradition enjoyed greater access.

- Other groups like the *Jamaat-e-Islami* were appointed to key industries.

- Shariat benches were established at high judiciary levels.[66]

Another change with implications for Pakistan's governance and future dealt with education. As Riedel writes, "one measure of this transformation was the enormous growth of Islamic schools, or *madrassas*. Between 1971 and 1988 their numbers multiplied from 900 to 8,000 official religious schools and another 25,000 unregistered ones. Under Zia, diplomas granted by *madrassas* became equivalent to university degrees. Their influence throughout Pakistan increased proportionately."[67]

Overall, Zia's shift to Islamic governance has deepened not only contention between secularists and the *ulama*, among others, but more centrally between the civilian governments and the military. The afore-mentioned leadership changes between civilian

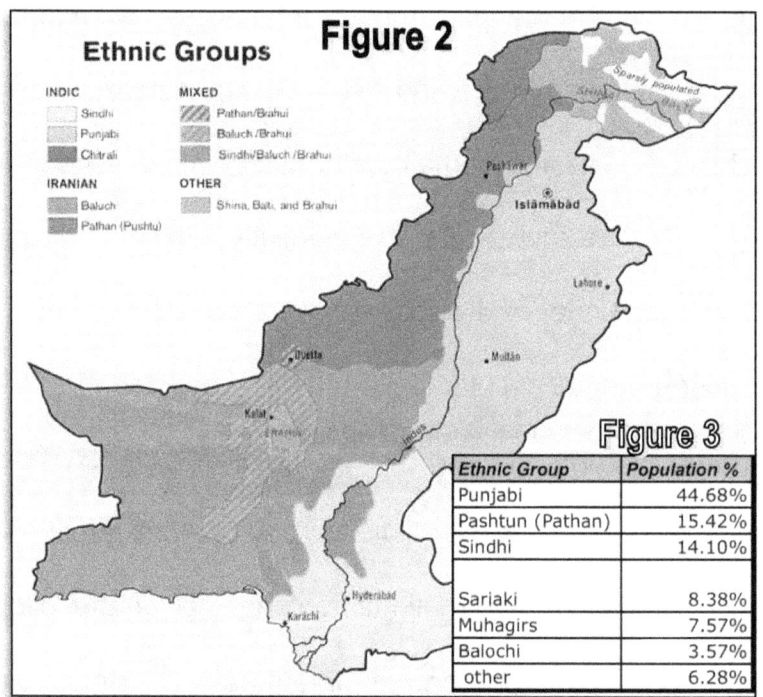

Figure: 2 & 3: Pakistan's Ethnic Groups (By Province and %)
(F2: Source: "Informed Consent, Thoughts on the Middle East, History and Religion.")
(F3: Source: "Ethnic groups by country," Nationmaster)

Ethnic Group	Population %
Punjabi	44.68%
Pashtun (Pathan)	15.42%
Sindhi	14.10%
Sariaki	8.38%
Muhagirs	7.57%
Balochi	3.57%
other	6.28%

authorities (secular) and the military (dominated by Islamic advocates, often in key positions) exemplifies the level to which the secular and Islamic ideologies continue to compete for dominance in national leadership.

Ideology in Pakistan is defined by two underlying variables: Ethno-linguistic and tribal/local leader influences. They are interrelated and make their way into Pakistani political and societal institutions and, with it, decision-making processes.

As *Figures 2*[68] and *3 (i.e., % of <u>total</u> population)*[69] illustrate, Pakistan's ethnic make-up is province-rooted and widely-varied throughout the nation. Yet, it is also dominated by at least six major ethnic groups, which define the socio-economic and political aspects of their respective provinces. For example, the Punjabi are located in the central-western province and, with it, dominate the area – including in Islamabad, the seat of government. The sheer numbers in the area – compounded by the deeply established norms and values of these centuries-old populations – create a distinct ethno-cultural identity and way of life favored over national ones. This distinction is further defined by language. In other terms, Urdu is Pakistan's "official language," yet only 8% of the total population speaks it. Pakistan's ethnic groups prefer to speak their own language, as exemplified by the Punjabi who make up over 44.6% of the total population. These ethnic and linguistic separations manifest cultures and beliefs (or ideologies) that can be at odds with those prescribed or encouraged through national governance. Thus, once again, the nation's "Islam" might not be that of certain ethnic groups and/or the provinces they dominate.

This separation also applies to the tribal areas, which are subsets of the provinces they inhabit. As indicated earlier, the relative isolation of tribes (governed by feudals and tribal leaders) has created challenges to economic development and national unity. Thus, national unity is expressed in only so far as it does not interfere with their cultural identity and even, in the case of Punjabi, their relative autonomy. This tribal and/or ethno-linguistic centralization within specific regions or provinces is perhaps, as Goodson noted, "the single most salient fact about Pakistan's ongoing penchant for domestic instability."[70]

So, what does this ethno-linguistic, cultural, and thus ideological diversity mean? In part, this has created a divided nation perhaps incapable of aligning itself under a singular, unified intellectual and religious identity. The result has been a contradictory, ideology-based governance, created by contesting visions, cultures, and government objectives. It has culminated in Pakistan's domestic instability and security concerns, creating pressures that have compelled internal and foreign policy decisions and behaviors. Further, this separation has created the need to protect certain ways of life, which include socio-economic and political interests as well. An example of this is the afore-mentioned feudalist participation in Parliament, in which they ensure that policies or laws (i.e., taxation) contrary to their interests are not implemented. Yet, a more overarching example, with national impacts, can be found in the East-West contention that eventually led to the cessation of East Pakistan in 1971.

As Riedel succinctly explains, West Pakistan was dominated (from the beginning) by the Punjab, which contained more resources than the Sindh, Baluchistan, the North-West Frontier Provinces, and the portion of Kashmir that joined Pakistan. However, most Pakistanis (56 percent) lived in East Pakistan, which included the Bengal territories that had been overlooked in the naming of Pakistan, reflecting its lesser importance. Jinnah saw Bengal as a separate state in which Muslims and Hindus could unite – one that could thus further weaken India. The largely Muslim section became East Pakistan, which became cut off from its capital – and center of power – Calcutta."[71]

As a result, the Bengalis were regarded as second-class citizens, without even their language considered to be legitimate by the state. Shortly after independence, Jinnah (from West Pakistan), opted solely for Urdu as the official language, stating that there would be "no other language" and those who did were "enemies of Pakistan . . . The Bengalis were outraged."[72] It was the first shot fired in an east-west dispute that would result in the 1971 split and creation of Bangladesh. It also exemplifies Pakistan's inability to establish democracy over cultural and ideological interests.

Pakistan's ideological – or religious – objectives have also spilled over into the Kashmir dispute. As *Figure 4* (depicting Kashmir's religious profile)[73] illustrates, there are twice the number of Muslims in Kashmir than any other religion. This reality has been the center of Pakistan's claims on the territory, as it was the only Muslim-dominated land not given to Pakistan at the partition. This was due to the unwillingness or inability of "Hari Singh, the autocratic maharaja of Kashmir," to decide whether to join India or Pakistan[74] when the British

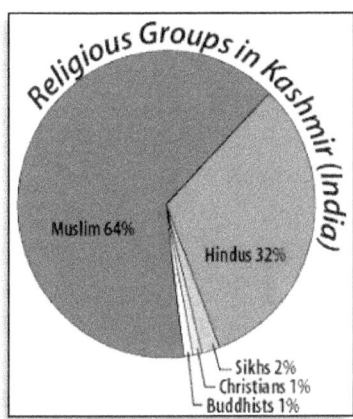

Figure 4: Kashmir Relgious Breakdown
(Source: "Kashmir and Its People," Global Perspectives)

Raj ended in 1947. His indecision triggered the onset of the on-going dispute. It has been the justification for two wars and the 1999 Kargil standoff. In the 1947-48 war, the government called on religious leaders to issue "fatwas" to galvanize forces to capture Kashmir. Today, Islamic radicals have become heavily involved in the dispute, including the presence of *Lashkar-e-Taiba* – enlisted directly by Zia – for use in Kashmir.[75]

Perhaps the most profound impact of Pakistan's ideological proliferation – separation – can be found in the rise of Islamic radicalism in Pakistan's tribal areas, particularly in North and South Waziristan. As of 2010, the Brookings Institute estimates that there are approximately 20-25,000 *Tehreek-e-Talibn Pakistan* (TTP)- or the Pakistan Taliban[76] – and numerous other Jihadi groups. These include: *Sipah-e-Sahaba Pakistan* (SSP), *Lashkar-e-Jhangvi* (LeJ),

Jaish-e-Mohammad (JeM), and *Lashkar-e-Taiba* (LeT) operating in the FATA, Punjab, and Swat valley (among other places). Recent estimates indicate that there could be as much as 156,000 Pakistan-based militants, with only a small fraction associated with *al Qaeda*.[77] However, the al Qaeda-affiliated *Haqqani Network* has increased in size and influence since 2009 and frequently attacks US-NATO positions in Afghanistan. Pakistan and the US believe that it harbors some of the world's most dangerous terrorists. It is obvious that, at least to some extent, such ideology-based radicalism is being grown in Pakistan.

In spite of the threats posed by domestically based terrorist groups, the Pakistani government – and military – can't or won't crackdown. Why? One clue might reside in a statement by former Foreign Secretary of Pakistan, Tanvir Khan. He believes that, "If the army does in North Waziristan what the Americans want it to do, overnight the *Haqqanis* become enemies of Pakistan . . . (However, it) 'would be a much harder nut to crack.' And, if the military were to dedicate its army to combating militants on its western border, it would risk leaving its eastern flank vulnerable to attack from India."[78] This is yet another example of how Islamic ideological considerations (this time, with a link to India) drive policy decisions. Driven by numerous interpretations of Islam, radicalism has proliferated, leading to ideological sympathies – and individual Islamic identities – in provinces increasingly incompatible with Pakistan's intended national one.

In 2002, Musharraf seemed to recognize the problem when he advocated an "Islamic ethos" called "enlightened moderation," stating:

> The first part is for the Muslim world to shun militancy and extremism and adopt a path of socio-economic uplift. The second is for the West, and the US in particular, to . . . resolve all political disputes with justice and to aid in the socio-economic betterment of the . . . Muslim world.[79]

Yet, his policy failed, "largely due to policies (empowering) the Islamic parties and (toleration of) militant groups."[80]

Currently, the existing Islamic-demographic ideological pressures threaten to further erode Pakistan's domestic and regional stability. Without the necessary domestic reforms (i.e., political, socio-economic), Pakistan will be unable to change or modify its foreign policy behavior to align with solutions that enhance – rather than undermine – regional stability. With the evolving "youth bulge (in which about "48% of Pakistan's population is under 20 years old and 67% is under 30")[81] and, with it, potential involvement in Islamic radicalism (due to discontent, poverty, and other factors) looming, Pakistan may encounter additional stability concerns.

As Haider writes, "Pakistan's viability as a state depends in large part on its ability to develop a new and progressive Islamic narrative."[82] Yet, based on the preceding, this is perhaps unlikely without the internal courage and leadership to make the needed reforms. Without them, Pakistan's policies and conduct will be impacted accordingly.

US-Pakistan (US-Pak) Relations: An Assessment

Because of intersecting regional interests, US relations remain an integral part of Pakistan's foreign policy. Thus, as this analysis will explore ways in which the US can positively impact the preceding factors, a brief assessment is in order.

The degree to which the US can influence the improvement of these factors is directly proportionate to its credibility and trustworthiness to both India and Pakistan. Yet, initially, it will depend on the overall status of US-Pak relations, common interests, and mutually perceived prospects for the future.

Issued in May 2010, the current US National Security Strategy (NSS) speaks to such interests and prospects:

We will foster a relationship with Pakistan founded upon mutual interests and mutual respect . . . We will strengthen Pakistan's capacity to target violent extremists within its borders, and . . . provide security assistance to support these efforts. To strengthen Pakistan's democracy and development, we will provide substantial assistance responsive to the needs of the Pakistani people, and sustain a long-term partnership committed to Pakistan's future.[83]

Despite the expressed intentions of both nations to seek common interests and partnership, US-Pak relations have been relatively inconsistent, with periods of estrangement followed by close mutual cooperation (as in the 1980s and 2001 through 2010). Understanding policy and behaviors largely depends on context, and the history of US-Pak relations provides a substantive one. This history will also provide clues to the potential future success of US-Pak relations.

The genesis of US-Pak relations stems from the Cold War. Following the partition, India aligned itself with the Soviet Union and, to counter, Pakistan aligned itself with the West. Because of its proximity to China and Central Asia, the US recognized its strategic importance and sought to make Pakistan a central agent in its "Containment" policy toward the Soviet Union. However, because it was primarily focused on rebuilding Europe after World War II and the Korean War, the Truman administration made only token efforts to move the relationship forward.

In 1953, President Dwight D. Eisenhower took the first substantive step and approved an initial an arms aid package, as he believed that an arms relationship and alliance with Pakistan would be strategically beneficial. "Ike established a relationship between Pakistan and the CIA that endures even today."[84] Ultimately, Ike would remark that Pakistan was "'America's most allied ally' in Asia.'"[85]

The US-Pak relationship continued to develop throughout the Eisenhower administration. In 1953, Army Chief of Staff Ayub Khan visited Washington with a request for more aid and to burnish the fledgling relations with face-to-face meetings with

President Eisenhower and Vice President Richard Nixon. In December 1953, Nixon returned the favor, effectively becoming the prime mover of US-Pak relations.

In 1955, Pakistan joined the US-backed *Southeast Asia Treaty Organization* (*SEATO*) and the *Central Treaty Organization* (*CENTO*) and developed a clandestine intelligence alliance that culminated in a classified air base in Peshawar, Pakistan in 1958. The US Air Force 6937th Communications Group (for U2 aerial reconnaissance), National Security Agency (NSA), and Central Intelligence Agency (CIA) used the base to monitor Chinese and Soviet activities.[86]

In 1961, President John F. Kennedy continued to seek better relations with both Pakistan and India. He hosted Khan for two state visits in 1961 and 1962; one at Mount Vernon (the only time a state dinner has been hosted there since Washington died), and the other at Kennedy's farm in Middlesex, Virginia. The relationship was tested when the Kennedy administration provided arms to India for the brief Indo-Chinese border (1962), but Kennedy assured Pakistan that it would not supplant US-Pak relations.[87]

The first blow came when President Lyndon B. Johnson suspended US aid to Pakistan for its role in the 1965 India-Pakistan war. Pakistan viewed this as a betrayal, and the unintended consequence of this was that Pakistan "approached . . . China for help (and it) would supplant the (US) as Pakistan's chief source of arms and in time would become its nuclear partner as well."[88]

Relations with Pakistan improved with the election of Nixon in 1968. In fact, Nixon approached Yahya Khan with the idea of Pakistan serving as an intermediary to facilitate direct American-Chinese contact. "For the next two years, Pakistan passed messages back and forth between Nixon and Mao."[89] However, during the 1971 war with India and East Pakistan, the US refused to provide military support – effectively "destroying

31

Pakistan's trust in the fidelity of the relationship."[90] Pakistan blamed its subsequent defeat in the conflict on the US, contending that its relationship with the US was generally useless if it chose to withhold support when pursuing its own domestic and foreign policy interests. The relationship became even more fragmented under President Jimmy Carter, who sought to sanction Pakistan for its pursuit of a nuclear program. As Riedel relates, "Carter, traveling to South Asia in 1977, visited India but flew over Pakistan to Iran. The message was clear: Pakistan and America were no longer allies."[91]

The relationship saw a restoration under President Ronald Reagan. After Zia rejected a Carter Administration $400 million aid package in exchange for supporting US efforts after the Soviets invaded Afghanistan (1979), Reagan re-approached Pakistan with an annual $500 million aid package. Reagan also sought to avoid the Carter administration's mistakes by ordering Secretary of State Alexander Haig "not to get into the details of the aid package until they had reached a satisfactory understanding on the issues of concern to Pakistan . . . including the 'nuclear problem,' and (US human rights policy) 'fault-finding'"[92] of the Carter years. Despite public opposition in Pakistan, the US-Pak cooperation in the 1980s proved essential to the Soviet defeat in Afghanistan.

In 1992, the imposition of the "Pressler Amendment," which prohibited the use of US aid for nuclear weapons development, triggered another decade of strained US-Pak relations. When President Bill Clinton did visit Pakistan in March 2000 for five hours, it was only after a five-day trip to India. Pakistan saw it as yet more evidence that "the (US) was fickle, unreliable, and not a true friend of Pakistan."[93]

The tragic events of 9/11 signaled a new period of US-Pakistan relations. Even as internal ideological contention mounted, Pakistan supported US operations with many consequential activities through 2010. These included: "operations that have led to the

32

capture of over 500 al Qaeda militants, (granting) US military access to bases within Pakistan, aiding in the identification and (capture) of extremists, (and) helping to seal the border between Pakistan and Afghanistan"[94]

The increasingly visible impasse within Pakistan over the US presence and support has made US-Pak relations again tenuous – especially after the 2011 Bin Laden raid. In fact, a 2011 Pew Research Center poll found that the "U.S remains viewed as an enemy to Pakistan by roughly 70% of the population. Less than 10% of the population views the U.S favorably."[95] Such findings necessitate an analysis of why this is the case. And, while the recent Kerry-Lugar Bill (which promises $1.5 Billion per year for ten years regardless of political changes) has been met with guarded optimism, the impasse continues – largely due to mistrust caused by past slights and internal ideological pressures.

As Iqbal states, "if Pakistan is to emerge from this conflict as a . . . stabilizing influence within the region, the (US) and Pakistan need to dispel their suspicions and reconcile differences." [96] Some believe that this should begin with a review of the current "AFPAK Policy," which has created ambivalence and contention within Pakistan's government and "intelligensia" circles.

According to the *US State Department Stabilization Strategy*, an objective of the current AFPAK Strategy is to pursue "a . . . 'whole of government' approach with the (US) 'leading the international community in helping Pakistan overcome the political, economic, and security challenges . . ."[97] While described as "an important first step toward . . . a viable regional strategy . . . it fails to recognize and adjust to the unique strategic and operational environments of each."[98] To many, it is largely Afghanistan-centric, linking the strategic approaches to both countries without accounting for their unique issues and concerns. For example, the strategy does not address on-going Indo-Pak concerns, and only mentions India in the context of its increasing involvement in Afghanistan (an important Pakistani concern).

It appears that at least two things need to occur to stabilize current US-Pak relations: foster a new climate of trust and cooperation, which would require consistency of behavior from both sides, and review the strategic policies of both nations toward one another to ensure they address each other's unique interests.

For the US, establishing renewed trust includes continuous engagement, keeping promises, and providing support even at considerable political risk. In other terms, the US and Pakistan must behave as allies and not merely as strategic partners tied to specific operations and goals. As demonstrated by the perceived abandonment of Pakistan after the Cold War was won, once such goals are realized, the alliance can lessen in importance, creating the estrangements that lead to mistrust and even adversarial relationships. As the preceding historical overview has indicated, US support for Pakistani interests has encountered intermittent periods of carelessness, neglect, and even contempt (i.e., the Carter years). Ultimately, US-Pak relational stability will require renewed support from pivotal governmental agencies and the Pakistani population, among others. This will require a new consistency with which the US manages its relations with Pakistan.

Pakistan must also mitigate US mistrust and review its own policy approach to the US and its interests. South Asia policy analysts Moeed Yusuf, Huma Yusuf, and Salman Zaidi provide their assessment:

> (Pakistan) . . . is seen as having responded to US actions in a manner that ensures continuation of the Pakistan-US partnership while securing Pakistani national security interests, as defined by the security establishment . . . While Islamabad has been critical of the lack of clarity in US policy, it has itself failed to articulate a coherent plan towards Afghanistan that allows for long-

34

term engagement on multiple levels . . . Pakistan has tried to balance . . . two competing aspects in its policy. It (continues to) provide counterterrorism and strategic . . . support to the (US) to ensure that Washington (engages) Pakistan as a partner . . . Simultaneously, Pakistan has refused to . . . aggressively target the Afghan Taliban and other Pakistan-based groups operating...from Pakistani territory."[99]

Currently, the view held by many is that Pakistan is generally tolerating (rather than fully supporting) US concerns and providing limited support while appeasing the Islamic extremists undermining regional stability. To foster US trust, Pakistan must dispel this view through salient action. One avenue would be to actually target the Pakistan-based insurgencies impacting Indo-Pak relations and US operations. Yet, as the Army's unwillingness to target such groups as the *Haqqani Network* exemplifies, there appears to be a lack of capacity or will to do so. To restore this Pakistan policy clarity – and trust from the US – the Pakistan government needs to be seen as making genuine efforts, to include enlisting an international or regional coalition to provide the capacity to fight if it does not have it. Like the US, Pakistan must also pursue consistent engagement, burnished through good faith efforts and honest dialogue, to restore the trust needed resolve issues – both internal and regional. Restoration of this trust would afford both sides with the credibility and perhaps popular leverage to resolve the complex and volatile issues plaguing Pakistan's domestic situation and overall regional stability. It would also provide a basis to improve US-Pak relations in the future.

Recommendations

There are significant measures the US can take to favorably affect these two overarching factors and facilitate improved regional and domestic security. Improving Pakistan's security and stability has profound implications for US policy and initiatives throughout the region. However, from a US standpoint, proposed recourses must also support its vital and important interests. Based on this analysis, these include:

35

Vital Interests: 1) Combat terrorism and extremists in Afghanistan and throughout the region; 2) Prevent war/armed conflicts between India and Pakistan; 3) Eliminate and/or greatly reduce nuclear weapon non-proliferation and threat of use between India and Pakistan; 4) Promote regional stability; 5) Achieve stability and the capacity for self-governance in Afghanistan.

Important Interests: 1) Improve overall economic (i.e., market access, trade), political, and cultural relations between India and Pakistan; 2) Partner with India and Pakistan to balance regional threats posed by China, Russia, and non-state belligerents (i.e., Taliban); 3) Establish long-term diplomatic engagement with South Asia.

These interests also converge with those of Pakistan, India, and other regional partners. For Pakistan, improving its security situation is the first step in protecting them.

<u>Factor One: Indo-Pak Relations</u>

"Indo-Pak relations" is a vital area where the US could help. Based upon their feasibility, acceptability, and suitability, potential courses of action (COA) are as follows:

COA #1: Comprehensive Diplomatic Engagement. The US should initiate comprehensive (i.e., social, political, economic) diplomatic engagement with both countries. As exemplified by the US role in resolving the Kargil conflict (1999), the US would facilitate bilateral and/or "back-channel" (clandestine) talks to resolve their disputes incrementally. Cultural exchanges like the "Friends without Borders" initiative (2006), in which numerous Indo-Pak children became pen pals, would connect populations at personal levels, improving social compatibility. The US should facilitate outreach efforts at all levels, including economic and humanitarian relief. Recent precedents include the 2001 Gujarat Earthquake (in India) and 2005 earthquake (Pakistan) in which both countries provided relief to the other. The US should partner with neighboring countries to

36

assist in outreach and mitigation of Indo-Pak issues.[100] The US could also provide military and US Homeland Security advisers to improve security programs in each country. The US should establish multi-faceted information campaigns, think tanks/ education forums through various governmental/non-governmental agents (i.e., universities, religious groups) and communities to promote greater understanding[101] of both countries and regional dynamics.

For this analysis, "risks" are defined as uncertain outcomes or potentially adverse developments created by actions taken. The risks associated with this COA include: a larger US diplomatic corps would be needed in the region, increasing costs. Also, perceptions of US "meddling" may prevail among social and political elements of both nations, potentially limiting US influence.

COA # 2: A Stand-Alone Kashmir Solution. The US should facilitate a resolution of the Kashmir dispute independent of other issues. The US Institute for Peace notes that "Kashmir remains the single most outstanding issue"[102] – or obstacle – to Indo-Pak normalization. The armed stand-off at the LOC and militant activities in and around Kashmir speak to its continuing volatility. However, a Kashmir resolution must originate from India and Pakistan, as third party involvement is generally resisted by India. Thus, the US could play a "back-channel," delicate role to promote viable compromises, including establishing an independent Kashmir state (present borders) or a sharing agreement of Kashmir's resources. The US should encourage regional partners (i.e., China, Russia, Bangladesh, etc.) to assist or pressure India and Pakistan compromises. In its public statements and negotiations, the US should promote the spirit of the 1972 *Simla* declaration, which mandated that both countries "settle their differences by peaceful means . . . mutually agreed upon between them."[103]

The risks associated with this COA include: insistence by the US of negotiating on Kashmir could alienate India, which is less willing to negotiate than Pakistan. China, which owns some of the historic lands, might block any settlement if it's not in its interests.

COA #3: Economic Incentive and Engagement. The US should facilitate the development and use of economic incentives and coercion (i.e., sanctions) to leverage a reduction of hostilities. The US should promote mutual economic interests and potential benefits of increased cooperation. Since 2001, both countries have experienced significant economic growth, but few more than India. Compared to the Pakistani economic situation, the open market Indian economy has a" $4.06T, 10.4% GDP Growth Rate, 478.3 million person labor Force 478.3M (#2 in the world) as of 2010."[104] Both have the same China, Saudi Arabia, and US as trading partners. The US should persuade these trading partners to pressure India and Pakistan to improve trade relations as well. The US should promote the use of economic sanctions and other punishments (i.e., trade status reduction, tying aid to diplomatic progress) if bilateral negotiations break down or hostilities ensue. The US should also encourage increased trade among NATO countries with both nations to enhance economic relations. Increasing mutual economic interests and success would potentially reduce tensions, enhancing domestic security and regional stability.

Potential risks include: added wealth could increase military spending for both countries, resulting in a regional arms race. Increased economic interdependence could discourage the use of sanctions (due to their impacts), lessening the effectiveness of economic power to encourage negotiations or punish aggression.

COA #4: Military Leveraging and/or "Peacekeeping Support." The US should facilitate the creation of a UN sanctioned coalition of regional and international partners (i.e., US, India, Pakistan, China, Bangladesh, Singapore, others) to provide humanitarian and/or peace-keeping in disputed territorial and border areas (i.e., Kashmir, LOC) to deter or mediate potential hostilities. The US should provide and/or facilitate diplomatic pressure and intelligence monitoring to ensure nuclear non-proliferation and stability.

Potential risks include: the presence of US and coalition forces might be viewed with distrust and opposition, creating an Iraq-like insurgencies or a larger regional war. Depending on the level of coalition involvement, this might become another US-centric operation – becoming costly and potentially harmful to US forces and regional relations.

COA #5: Kashmir Solution and Economic Engagement. The US should pursue a Kashmir resolution (independent of other Indo-Pak issues) and use of economic incentives and coercion (i.e., sanctions) to reduce hostilities. Regarding "Kashmir Solution," the US should pursue constructive and covert diplomatic engagement to establish balanced Indo-Pak negotiations to resolve the Kashmir question. The US should encourage both countries to break down the Kashmir question into salient issues and negotiate each one of them separately. Due to its complexity and intractability, the issue cannot be solved holistically. A deliberate and incremental approach is needed to create "small wins" that contribute to a larger agreement. The US should facilitate and promote economic interdependence through increased trade, agricultural and industrial initiatives to elevate each nation. Economic prosperity is vital to internal stability and external viability, and both nations would benefit. Key openings in these areas could create openings for greater cooperation in the future.

Potential risks include: even constructive diplomatic US engagement could alienate India, or it might not be enough to leverage meaningful change. Increased economic power and mutual interests might not be enough to diffuse Indo-Pak mistrust and intransigence, effectively creating greater means for both nations to wage war.

Recommendation: *COA #5*: Kashmir Solution and Economic Engagement.

Because Kashmir is the driving sub-factor in Indo-Pak relations, resolving it would provide a key basis on which to resolve other less severe border disputes. "Washington has been more effective at crisis management than peace building in Kashmir. The dispute has stubbornly resisted the diplomatic efforts of outside powers, even when the US) enjoyed great leverage."[105] Yet, an incremental approach and continued engagement could improve the US record. The US needs to be consistent in achieving the solution and remaining engaged in its aftermath. According to Schaffer, "Pakistan has long acknowledged that it is willing to settle for less than the whole state. It will be satisfied with the transfer of the valley to its control. (India) has implied (since the 1950s) and even explicitly acknowledged that it is prepared to give up . . . the territories now administered by the Pakistanis and accept the line that divides . . . as an international boundary."[106] Also, in 2008, trade resumed between Pakistani and Indian-controlled parts of Kashmir – the first such exchange in 60 years.[107] Thus, negotiating positions and precedents already exist and can be cultivated to a possible solution. It would be the first and most important domino to fall in the Indo-Pak stalemate, bringing to a close an impasse that has plagued the nations since 1947. Resolution would significantly reduce tensions and probably the likelihood of hostilities. While the risks cited in Options 2, 3, and 5 are valid, they are less likelihood with a "back-channel" and constructive US role. Indo-Pak leaders would be less pressured by anti-US bias among internal actors and could conceivably be more willing to discuss Kashmir-related issues with less political distraction. Such an approach – if successful – could also foster trust for the US and open other diplomatic avenues in the future.

However, continued diplomatic viability would depend on a concerted US effort to maintain engagement throughout the process, and mitigate the on-going mistrust of the Pakistanis. Economically, mutual interests and interdependence are natural deterrents to radical behaviors and policies that could jeopardize relations. Economic prosperity equates to domestic and global progress, and greater means to higher standards of living. Thus, a "Win-Win" financial situation is mutually attractive, and could encourage a more disciplined co-existence between the two nations. Positively impacting this factor would promote Indo-Pak security, regional stability, and preserve US-Indo-Pak interests.

Factor Two: Ideology

Because Pakistan's evolution has created a fragmented national Islamic-ideological narrative, it is arguably the most difficult factor to change. The focus should not be on holistically trying to change or even judge the ideology – or Islam – itself. This could be construed as an attack on the religion, inducing more anti-US propaganda. Rather, solutions must address the ideological rationale used to justify violence or nefarious activities, while applying practical measures to deter future recurrences. Solutions could include: building security capacity, cultural outreach (i.e., education), and infiltrating remote areas to counter radicalism and create conditions conducive to socio-economic reforms. Dialogue must complement practical measures to answer extremist propaganda so misconceptions can be corrected, altering future behavior. However, in Pakistan, all non-military measures must be leveraged by military means to ensure the security needed for success. Based on the preceding, potential courses of action (COA) are as follows:

COA #1: Indo-Pak Détente. The US should facilitate an Indo-Pak peace agreement to divert military forces from Pakistan's eastern border and deploy a UN capacity-building/security building force. Pakistani forces would use its "freed up" forces for intraprovincial policing actions, concentrating on one province and/or dominant militant group at a time while building capacity through partnering with the UN partners. This UN-sanctioned force would include economic, humanitarian, and limited peacekeeping/military elements to support building homeland security systems and socio-economic improvements. To mitigate opposition (to the agreement and UN force) from powerful Islamists throughout Pakistan, additional security capacity should be built through clandestine US/NATO-Pakistani intelligence and special operations. This may include deploying a force to Kashmir and/or along the LOC to deter Indian or Pakistan-based Islamic militant activities designed to undermine progress. The use of aerial drones would be vital to monitor activities. Persuade China and Russia to support using economic and political incentives to enforce the peace agreement, and support UN security building operations.

Potential risks include: collapse of the Indo-Pak agreement would make the other measures infeasible and could risk another conflict in Kashmir. Also, intervention from militant groups outside of Pakistan and even from Iran could ignite a full-scale insurgent war, destroying Pakistan's domestic security.

COA #2: Reject Radicalism. The US should initiate a popular and clandestine civil-military and information operations program to encourage rejection of radicalism. The information campaign would focus only on extremist propaganda and be pursued by civil-military leaders and through clandestine information operations activities. Civil-military leaders would incrementally establish population-focused media/education campaigns to refute Islamic radicalism nation-wide and would be designed to empower secularists and populations at local levels. It would include education in mosques (i.e., relating it to the Quran), and provincial/international cultural exchanges. This could include student

42

exchanges from western colleges and greater access of humanitarian organizations to build and teach in Pakistani schools. Clandestine activities would be established in hostile tribal/feudal areas. Military support would be required to identify and eliminate those leaders obstructing reforms or inciting radical activities from their areas. The ISI and US-NATO intelligence services would pursue the clandestine campaign. The campaign would also disseminate information to galvanize grass-roots popular support for socio-economic reforms and refute Islamist propaganda. Like the information campaigns waged by the US, UK, and the Vatican against Soviet domination in Eastern Europe in the 1980s, the campaign would be directed to local populations to win the "hearts and minds" needed to reject Islamic radicalism. Without popular support, radicalism would be weakened – creating a gradual reduction of influence throughout Pakistan.

Potential risks include: radicals could initiate their own information or popular persecution campaigns, igniting more armed conflict and undermining the viability of the program. "Pro-democracy-secularist" messages could be turned against the West as another ploy to extend its domination over Islam, making US-western influence appear suspect or negligible.

COA #3: Socio-Economic Progress. The US should create a US-led international coalition of non-military humanitarian and economic organizations to build socio-economic reforms and facilitate progress. This initiative would be designed to provide socio-economic assistance nation-wide irrespective of politics. Again, a Pakistani military and/or UN-sanctioned security force would be needed to protect participants from militant attacks. Humanitarian organizations could provide infrastructure construction, medical, and education/literacy programs, among others. Civic and business leaders can provide instruction or advice on building markets, industries, and affecting overall economic growth. Overall, this approach emphasizes humanistic or "quality of life" deeds over ideological and political considerations. Directed at the indigenous populations, it would foster sympathy and perhaps trust with the west – reducing perceptions of US-European fickleness or unreliability as allies.

Potential risks include: depending on the level of support, this could become another very costly US-led humanitarian mission. Also, without the proper armed security, such non-military actors would be a great risk to militant attack.

COA #4: Reject Radicalism and Achieve Socio-Economic Progress. The US should pursue limited versions of COAs #2 and #3, emphasizing an incremental approach to establishing both programs gradually over time. For example, the clandestine information campaign described above could be instituted gradually into more stable provinces and expanded as conditions allow. As the campaign strengthens popular resolve, civil-military leaders can more openly advocate support for reforms with less risk of militant propaganda and/or armed interference. The information campaign should be introduced *after* the initiation and acceptance of the US-led non-military coalition described in COA #3 (i.e., *Socio-economic Progress*) to lessen popular resistance to the anti-radical/pro-democracy values of the information campaign. Also, emphasizing the humanitarian activities and ignoring ideological or political considerations would promote them as "neutral" enterprises, potentially mitigating militant fervor and achieving some of the intent of the "Reject Radicalism" COA. Again, the demonstration of such values – like all deeds – can be instructive and credible if they lead to positive results. The population needs to believe the efforts and motivations are sincere before it believes the US and others are no longer its enemies. Potential risks include those described in COAs #2 and 3 above.

Recommendation: *COA #4*: Reject Radicalism and Achieve Socio-Economic Progress.

It is infeasible and unrealistic to anticipate affecting this factor quickly. Ideological extremism cannot be discredited or transformed through simple logic or coercion in the long term. Its rejection requires consequential activities and counter-arguments designed to subvert those elements that reinforce its perceived truthfulness to fundamentally transform thought. For a population like Pakistan's, it is perhaps as impossible to eradicate Islamic extremism as it is to eliminate misconception or bigotry itself. Radical Islam is antithetical to the religion of Islam itself, and is as pernicious to popular welfare as it is to domestic and global stability. Yet, the roots of radicalism run deep in Pakistan and, like most scourges or tyrannies, it has demonstrated a talent for resiliency and survival. This COA incrementally addresses the current challenges in changing "hearts and minds" confined by isolated geography, limited economic means, and centuries of religious exploitation (and thus misconception). It is a conservative approach to impacting ideological volatility with significant steps to improve lives, thus undermining the desperate circumstances under which radicalism flourishes. It demonstrates true awareness and dedication to the Pakistanis with manageable risk.

Conclusion

This analysis contains no illusions about the expediency or ease with which these factors can be changed to lasting effect. While each has evolved from conditions created in 1947, their genesis lies in the historic roots established by cultural migrations centuries ago. Thus, they are ancient factors impacting present conditions and future prospects. And, it will take generations to change the attitudes needed for real transformation.

The preceding recommendations suggest not only practical solutions but new perspectives on how to view these factors and what must be considered to affect them.

45

Their prudent and incremental employment could positively impact the state of Indo-Pak relations, mitigate the corrosive effects of Islamic radicalism in societal and institutional behaviors, and eventually improve stability. The US involvement could ensure lasting and constructive engagement, creating the trust needed for improved US-Pak relations. Like all problem solving, real progress begins with new or reconsidered perspectives designed to see problems as they are and aligning the means to mitigate their development and future impacts. Such new perspectives must partner with determined efforts to achieve lasting domestic and regional stability. These recommendations represent faithful efforts to this end.

The perspectives and efforts they present could, one day, facilitate a brighter future for Pakistan as a nation and US-Pakistan relations overall.

Endnotes

[1] *National Security Strategy of the United States.* The White House: Washington DC, May 2010, 4

[2] Malik Zafar Iqbal. *An Appraisal of the Afghanistan-Pakistan Strategy to Counter-Terrorism.* Parameters (Summer 2010). Carlisle, PA: US Army War College, 17

[3] Larry P. Goodson. "The Five Determinants of Pakistan." Strategic Research Article (provided by the author), US Army War College. Carlisle Barracks, PA, 2011, 1

[4] Barbara Metcalf and Thomas Metcalf. *A Concise History of Modern India (Cambridge Concise Histories)*, Cambridge and New York: Cambridge University Press, 2006, 221-222

[5] Islamic Republic of Pakistan," Encyclopedia of the Nations, Retrieved December 27, 2011 from http://www.nationsencyclopedia.com/economies/Asia-and-the-Pacific/Pakistan.html

[6] K. Alan Kronstadt. "*Pakistan: Key Current Issues and Developments* (June 1, 2010)," Congressional Research Service, retrieved December 12, 2011, from http://www.fas.org/sgp/crs/row/R41307.pdf

[7] Goodson, 5

[8] Ibid

[9] Goodson, 6

[10] Goodson, 7

[11] Goodson, 7-8

[12] Owen Bennett Jones. *Pakistan: Eye of the Storm* (Third Edition). New Haven: Yale University Press, 2009, 7

[13] Peter Blood. "Linguistic and Ethnic Groups." Pakistan: A Country Study. Washington: GPO for the Library of Congress, 1994.
[14] Goodson, 1

[15] "Pakistan." *Central Intelligence Agency: The World Fact Book*, Retrieved November 7, 2011 from https://www.cia.gov/library/publications/the-world-factbook/geos/pk.html

[16] Anthony H. Cordesman and Robert Hammond. "The Military Balance in Asia: 1990-2010: A Quantitative Analysis." *Center for Strategic and International Studies*. Washington DC, 2010, retrieved on November 8, 2011 from http://csis.org/files/publication/100914_AsiaMilitary Balance2010.pdf, 94

[17] Jones, 285-286

[18] B. Raman. "Saving Pakistan from its 'Saviors,'" *South Asian Analysis Group*, retrieved December 28, 2011, from http://www.southasiaanalysis.org/%5Cpapers2%5Cpaper151.html

[19] Jones, 57, 309-310

[20] "Pakistan." *Central Intelligence Agency: The World Fact Book*

[21] Jones, 250

[22] Ibid.

[23] Jones, 251

[24] Jones, 252-256

[25] "Pakistan." *Central Intelligence Agency: The World Fact Book*

[26] Iftikhar Malik. *Pakistan: Democracy, Terrorism, and the Building of a Nation*. Northampton, MA: Olive Branch Press, 2010, 28-31

[27] Malik, 31

[28] Bruce Riedel. *Deadly Embrace: Pakistan, America and the Future of Global Jihad*. Washington DC: Brookings Institution Press, 2011, 4. "A former CIA officer, Riedel was a senior advisor to four US presidents on South Asian issues," and "chaired an interagency policy review on Afghanistan and Pakistan" policy for President Obama, completed in March 2009 (taken from back cover flyleaf).

[29] Riedel, 4

[30] Ibid.

[31] Riedel, 4-5

[32] Haider, Ziad. *The Ideological Struggle for Pakistan*. Stanford: Hoover Institution Press, 2010, 4

[33] Riedel, 5

[34] Riedel, 6

[35] Riedel, 8

[36] Ibid.

[37] Ibid.

[38] Riedel, 9

[39] Riedel, 10

[40] Ibid.

[41] Riedel, 19

[42] Haider, 20

[43] Haider, 21

[44] Riedel, 27-28

[45] "Story of Pakistan: A Multimedia Journey," *Enterprise Team Website*, retrieved December 13, 2011, from http://www.storyofpakistan.com/ person.asp?perid=P029

[46] "Pakistan: In Depth Timeline," *CBC News*, retrieved December 13, 2011, from http://www.cbc.ca/news/background/ pakistan/

[47] Ian S. Livingston and Michael O'Hanlon. "Pakistan Index: Tracking Variables of Reconstruction & Security (November 29, 2011)," retrieved December 17, 2011, from www.brookings.edu/~/media/Files/Programs/FP/... /index.pdf, 4

[48] Ian S. Livingston and Michael O'Hanlon, 6-7

[49] Shirin Keen. "The Partition of India," *Emory College* (Website), retrieved December 17, 2011, from http://english.emory.edu/Bahri/Part.html

[50] Shirin Keen, from http://english.emory.edu/Bahri/Part.html

[51] Shirin Keen, from http://english.emory.edu/Bahri/Part.html

[52] "Kashmir and Its People," *Global Perspectives: A Remote Sensing and World Issues Site*, retrieved December 14, 2011, from http://www.cotf.edu/earthinfo/ sasia/kashmir/KAtopic1.html

[53] Howard B. Schaffer. *The Limits of Influence: America's Role In Kashmir.* Washington DC: Brooking Institution Press, 2009, 2

[54] Wajahat Habibullah. "The Political Economy of the Kashmir Conflict: Opportunities for Economic Peacebuilding and for U.S. Policy." United States Institute of Peace (website), retrieved December 28, 2011, from http://www.usip.org/publications/political-economy-kashmir-conflict-opportunities-economic-peacebuilding-and-us-policy

[55] Schaffer,1

[56] Haider, 8

[57] Riedel, 9

[58] Ibid.

[59] "Timeline: Conflict over Kashmir," CNN World (website), retrieved December 15, 2011 from http://articles.cnn.com/2003-02-06/world/ kashmir.timeline_1_india-and-pakistan-indian-military-officials-kargil?_s=PM: asiapcf

[60] Iqbal, 23

[61] Ibid.

[62] Haider, 3

[63] Ibid.

[64] Haider, 5

[65] Haider, 6

[66] Haider, 21

[67] Riedel, 21

[68] "Informed Consent, "Thoughts on the Middle East, History and Religion," Retrieved 7 December 2011 from http://www.juancole.com/2010/12/map-pakistan-ethnic-groups.html/pakistan_ethnic-2

[69] "Ethnic groups (most recent) by country," Nationmaster.com, retrieved December 7, 2011, from http://www.nationmaster.com/graph/peo_eth_gro-people-ethnic-groups (As of Mar 11)

[70] Goodson, 5

[71] Riedel, 6-7

[72] Riedel, 7

[73] "Kashmir and Its People," *Global Perspectives: A Remote Sensing and World Issues Site*, retrieved December 14, 2011, from http://www.cotf.edu/earthinfo/sasia/kashmir/KAtopic1.html

[74] Shaffer, 10-11

[75] Haider, 24

[76] Ian S. Livingston and Michael O'Hanlon, 4

[77] Ian S. Livingston and Michael O'Hanlon, 4

[78] Baker, 41-42

[79] Haider, 31

[80] Haider, 33

[81] Goodson, 14

[82] Haider, 1

[83] *National Security Strategy of the United States*, 21

[84] Riedel, 12

[85] Iqbal, 15

[86] Riedel, 13

[87] Riedel, 14

[88] Riedel, 15

[89] Ibid.

[90] Iqbal, 15

[91] Riedel, 27

[92] Dennis Kux. *The United States and Pakistan 1947-2000: Disenchanted Allies*. Washington DC: Woodrow Wilson Center Press, 2001, P.257-258

[93] Kux, 320

[94] Iqbal,18

[95] Faheem Haider. "New Public Opinion Poll Shows Decreased Support for Political Institutions in Pakistan," Foreign Policy Association, retrieved December 18, 2011, from http://foreignpolicyblogs.com/2011/06/21/support-for-political-institutions-in-pakistan-plunge-new-public-opinion-data-show/

[96] Iqbal, 14

[97] Iqbal, 19

[98] Iqbal, 29

[99] Moeed Yusuf, Huma Yusuf, Salman Zaidi. "Pakistan, the United States and the End Game in Afghanistan." The Jinnah Institute and the United States Institute of Peace, 2011, 28-29

[100] Glardon, Thomas L.. "Balancing U.S. Interests Amidst The India and Pakistan Conflict," *Strategic Research Project,* US Army War College. Carlisle Barracks, PA, 2011, Retrieved November 8, 2011, from http://www.strategicstudiesinstitute.army.mil/pdffiles/ksil12.pdf, 9

[101] Glardon, 11

[102] Moeed Yusuf. "On the Issues: US-Pakistan-India." United States Institute of Peace, retrieved November 7, 2011 from http://www.usip.org/publications/the-issues-us-pakistan-india

[103] Rahul Roy-Chaudhury. "The United States' Role and Influence on the India-Pakistan Conflict," retrieved on November 8, 2011 from http://www.unidir.org/pdf/articles/pdf-art2117.pdf, 37

[104] India" *Central Intelligence Agency: The World Fact Book*, Retrieved November 7, 2011 from https://www.cia.gov/library/ publications /the-world-factbook/geos/in.html

[105] Schaffer, 7

[106] Schaffer, 3

[107] "History of Pakistan," *Yellow Pages of Pakistan*, Retrieved December 13, 2011, from http://www.findpk.com/Pakistan/html/history.html